Adventures Of

A Dogsledding Diva

Adventures Of

A Dogsledding Diva

Doreen E. Wolff

authorHOUSE®

AuthorHouse™
1663 Liberty Drive
Bloomington, IN 47403
www.authorhouse.com
Phone: 1-800-839-8640

© 2012 by Doreen E. Wolff. All rights reserved.

No part of this book may be reproduced, stored in a retrieval system, or transmitted by any means without the written permission of the author.

Published by AuthorHouse   11/19/2012

ISBN: 978-1-4772-9016-3 (sc)
ISBN: 978-1-4772-9014-9 (e)

Library of Congress Control Number: 2012921439

Any people depicted in stock imagery provided by Thinkstock are models, and such images are being used for illustrative purposes only.
Certain stock imagery © Thinkstock.

This book is printed on acid-free paper.

Because of the dynamic nature of the Internet, any web addresses or links contained in this book may have changed since publication and may no longer be valid. The views expressed in this work are solely those of the author and do not necessarily reflect the views of the publisher, and the publisher hereby disclaims any responsibility for them.

Table of Contents

Chapter One

Building the Team

My first experience, in 1996, with dog sledding was to acquire a lab husky cross puppy that was on her way to being put down at the local animal shelter in Dawson Creek, B. C. I am an Early Childhood Educator and was working at as preschool teacher at Northern Lights College in Dawson Creek. I had been doing this for the past twelve years. My husband and I, own our small farm, three quarter sections of land, about sixteen miles west of Dawson Creek. I decided to take this little black puppy home never knowing, she would be a great leader and a dog with more heart for running in the harness than was good for her. Even as a puppy, she had exceptional strength, stamina, and intelligence. The first thing I did was name her, "Takla" after a old lake in the north, meaning free spirit, a perfect name for the great leader she would become.

I started by teaching her simple commands such as "sit" "down" and hopefully "stay." She also learned "no." I tried to instill good manners and discourage her from chewing everything from picnic tables to extension cords. At ten months old I started to harness break her. She took to it like a duck to water. She looked forward to training because it increased her freedom and she loved the little adventures we went on in the woods. We went every day, as she was crazy to go, and I also enjoyed the freedom after a long day working with young children. This became our escape into the world of wildlife and wilderness. This was our retreat into solitude and many wonderful adventures.

Takla slowly proved herself to be a steady, very fast worker. She learned immediately the meaning of the word "hike." Hike means mush or go and most dogs have an easy time with this command. Stopping is much harder to learn as a voice command. If your dogs are not trained to stop, they will only stop if you physically halt them. Some dogs will not listen to you if they realize you cannot control them. If you give up and let them go on, you are reinforcing bad behavior. This tells them it is okay to ignore your commands. I found with this little girl, praising her when she responded correctly, was really valuable. I found that patience, and being reasonable and gentle were my best assets. I feel pups are like the young children I work with, patience and consistency are vital. My goal was to make this girl a reliable, dependable leader, then add others after she was trained or it would be like the ignorant leading the uninitiated. I found it takes a lot of determination to try sledding without any outside help, so I went to the local library and read up on several different ways to train.

Takla soon developed a trotting gait. She could without any effort, go for miles at a lithe dynamic trotting pace. She also learned to pace naturally without fatigue or pain. She had a very keen interest to get on the trail and work.

As a recreational musher I began looking for other dogs to add to my excursions. My next dog I picked up on "death row," at the local shelter in Dawson Creek. The staff was happy to see me of course, and had a sweet little silky Eskimo dog (Greenland husky) for me. She had a scrappy personality and was a real follower which went well with Takla who was a bossy leader. I named her Trixie and she fit the position of second dog in swing really well. She was in good health, vaccinated and had good feet. I harnessed her with Takla and liked the combination. After a trial period and letting her adjust to what was expected, I was pleased with her ability to work. She adjusted to her new home and new comrade very quickly and followed Takla's lead well. She was not wildly excitable like the leader, nor was she too quiet or subdued. She seemed a good fit to build the team.

The next dog to come was my very best friend Yacoom, a malamute husky. I had been watching the local news casts and saw him advertised by the local SPCA. Another dog on "death row," that was very well bred but the owner could not care for him any longer. The owner was a very personable older gentleman of Hungarian heritage and thought the dog looked like a raccoon with his masked markings of black over his eyes. Hence, the name Yacoom as this is how the gentleman pronounced raccoon. Yacoom was a big strong dog, loved me with undying love, an excellent watch dog, and turned into an outstanding wheel dog. It took a lot of endurance training to get Yacoom ready for the trail, as he was not use to the strenuous exercise. I began by letting him run with the team unharnessed, to build up endurance and stamina. There was no need to teach this dog commands as he knew many (stay, sit, etc.) He tried eagerly to pick up our new commands of gee (go right), haw (go left) hike (go), and come gee (go full right turn), come haw (full left turn), and all my personal commands. He became my admirer and would do almost anything I wanted. He fit in with my other dogs and I was finding out how important it was to have a cohesive well adjusted team. I also learned very quickly that a musher HAS to be in command of their dogs. As a new musher without experience, my dogs did in effect teach me, the musher, what worked and what did not.

Then along came another opportunity. My married daughter phoned from Yellowknife, Yukon, telling me she was at the end of her rope with her dog Tundra. This dog was a full sister to my leader dog Takla. Tundra was not getting enough exercise or attention, living in the town of Yellowknife and my daughter eight months pregnant with her third child was unable to have enough time to spend with the dog. I hesitated a bit in deciding whether Tundra was sled dog material, as she had not been raised to run like her sister Takla. I finally decided if she was HALF the dog her sister was she would still be a good team dog. The process to break her in began as soon as she arrived from Yellowknife. I hooked her in tandem on the swing with little Trixie (Eskimo dog). We had a great many tangles and the pecking order had to be scrapped out daily for awhile, but eventually, a respectful peace settled on the team. I breathed a sigh of relief and was quite happy with the results.

These four dogs were the main team members. I ran other dogs with them but they never lasted as long as my fantastic foursome. I tried other dogs that did not fit in or want to work. Some enjoyed the harness and others did not. I ran a dog named Toby for quite some time with the team. His previous owners said he was half wolf. Toby was a lazy dog and didn't do his share of the work. If a dog does not pull, has never pulled, and never will pull, he is just a freeloader. Some animals simply cannot or will not work in a harness. Eventually I gave him to another home. The family I gave him to wanted a yard dog and they seemed pleased with him. I think my hard working dogs were just as glad to see the tail end of lazy Toby as I was.

I ran my dogs in summer as well as in winter. My husband Carl and I were soon learning how to manufacture training sleds, durable dog sleds, and three wheel carts. Along with books, trial and error, and my helpful but sometimes bizarre suggestions, we were finally on the trail to some of the biggest adventures of my life.

Chapter Two

Rigging out a sled, gear, and equipment

After getting the dogs trained for voice command, the next thing I needed was gear and a sled. The harness and lines were acquired by mail order from an equipment shop in the Yukon. Prices were very reasonable. I had borrowed a catalogue from a local teenage boy who had some experience with sled dogs. I ordered lots of lines and thought I could make what I needed as I went along. The harnesses I ordered through Tanzilla Harness Company in the Yukon. They were appropriate and fit the dogs well. For a harness to work it should lie smoothly over the dog without pinching or twisting. It should fit smoothly over the shoulders and not press on the throat. It should be padded in places of strain or it will cause sores and pain. This would make the dog reluctant to pull. The harness I used was made of flat, soft, one inch nylon webbing and was padded around the armpits and neck. For the towline I used a very strong piece of rope made of polyethylene which is durable and inexpensive. I also used brass swivel snaps and long tuglines so the dogs would not crowd each other. The necklines were approximately fourteen inches so when a tangle happened they were easy to sort out.

I now needed a sled big enough to train about three dogs at one time. My goal was to put my smart little leader,and well trained strong dogs, with the newer greener dogs and mold them into a united team. This is an awesome task. I did not want anything too heavy, but wanted the dogs to get use to the idea of me being pulled and giving directions from behind. I really needed a light, maneuverable sled that pulled easily with my weight on it.

My husband Carl and I thought about this for some time. We came up with a plan. We decided that a pair of downhill skis from the sixties, (found in the local dump) an old heavy fishnet, (found on the banks of the Murray River) a lot of metal tubing and small pipe, and last but by no means least, a plan in my husband's head. I had some difficulty with the plan as the only blueprint was in my husband's head. He did not discuss much with me and began undertaking the task to create this invention of a training sled. He always comes up with something that magically works well. I did look in his ear, but did not see much of anything, which worried me a bit.

This first training sled frame was made out of metal tubing, and we tied on pieces of the heavy fishnet to make a basket. We bolted down the downhill skis underneath to make a crude type of runners. At the back like a regular dogsled, is where I stood, on the runners, with a very small brake supplied by an old piece of grader blade and a heavy tarp strap. Now we were ready for training in basic form. Training involved me knowing what to do and the dogs knowing what I wanted them to do. It was primarily a painful tedious task, but as I gained knowledge and the dogs caught on and understood, we actually started going on trips down into our bottom valley. This jury rigged sled worked similar to skijoring and was light and therefore perfect for younger or inexperienced dogs and drivers as it did not sour them on too heavy of a pull. This sled gave the driver close proximity to the dogs, much better to bond and train. We all felt like a unit because we were so close together. Another advantage was that this little sled was so light it was easily transported if you wanted to truck the team to a different location or trail. This sled certainly trained the driver to improve her balance and I learned the hard way what happens when you do not have your weight evenly distributed.

On a fast downhill journey I dislocated my little finger. My first thought upon seeing my finger being horribly disfigured was, "Oh no, now I'll have to put the dogs away, and drive twenty miles to a doctor." The dog sledding angel was looking out for me as I grabbed off my gloves and held on tightly to the joint of the finger. Amazingly I heard a snap, and it was back in place. I continued down the trail as if nothing occurred. The next two weeks my hand looked terrible with dark bruising, but it didn't hurt. When asked what happened, I would just say "training." My co-workers were impressed and figured I was getting "tough as nails." The beauty of this training sled was that it could be used with one dog or three. It really was a great contraption to voice train dogs while pulling something.

The next sled I used was designed from a library book. My sled needed to maneuver easily and track in a straight line. The runners needed to be flexible enough to bend when cornering and absorb shock. We built my sled a bit narrower in front as the book stated that this helped the sled track better. We had birch wood on hand. It is a nice light wood and is shock-resistant if you hit rocks or a tree.

The handlebow, was rounded and we adjusted it to my height. If it is too high it is difficult to control the sled, and if it is too low it causes shoulder and back fatigue. To get the curve we steamed the wood in a clever contraption my husband built. He used a large metal pipe filled with water and heated with a torch. We also used this procedure for the brush bow. We purchased teflon plastic for the runners at a local hardware store and used screws to attach it to the runners. This teflon plastic lasted for many years, as I was not on gravel or abrasive trails very often. I talked with experienced mushers and they tell me that after fifty below, NOTHING glides better than green birch runners. I loved the traditional look of this birch sled. It had a great deal of grace and beauty.

I have tried out several snow hooks but found I did not need them too often. During wildlife sightings they were put to good use, as I found it difficult to anchor the team around elk and moose.

I decided I loved the winter sledding so much that I wanted to run my dogs in summer as well, so we set about building a dog cart. This would keep the dogs fit year round. The one we made was a real shock absorber and weighed about forty pounds. Ingenuity has resulted in the design of this light weight, wonderful cart. We used the back wheels and brakes of an old mini motorbike. Our dog cart had one wheel in front for precise turning. This dog cart was low and wide for stability. It had an uncanny ability to stay upright during all conditions. Rocks, stumps, and uneven terrain did not make this cart tip. It withstood vibrations and the brakes locked when you stopped. There was no problem efficiently controlling the dogs.

I, being a girl use to working with children and wearing a dress was in for a bit of a culture shock. I would be in such a rush to go "carting" with the dogs that I would leave the dress on and just put on a pair of sneakers. I would quickly harness the dogs and we would be off on the cart for another adventure. The dogs were as ready as I was and a high degree of excitement awaited me every afternoon. Co-workers at the college were wondering about my sanity and whether I had been working with children too long. I stayed the course with all their teasing and now started, was hooked. My country neighbors' nick named me "Diva" after seeing me flash by in a dress. Sometimes I would see a vehicle pulled over in a field or wooded area not believing how fast the "diva' could go driving dogs. This instigated a bit of showing off on my part, and off I would go yelling "hike." Then as we were going along at an incredibly fast pace, I would give the command "gee" or "haw" (left or right) and we would turn very sharply. On occasion this bit of showing off would lead to a mistake in judgment, on my behalf, or the dogs, and for the next few runs I would be a very humble driver indeed, until a bit of vanity struck again, usually when we had learned something new, I thought was very cool. Sometimes my friends stopped on the road entranced watching the "diva,' covered in mud (still with her dress on) from splashes from the creek bed and puddles from the rain, roaring down the trail like she was in a different world. I certainly enjoyed the freedom and experiences that this wonderful hobby led me to.

Chapter Three

Exploding Prairie Chickens

On a fine winter day, I arrived home from work at the preschool. I put on my snowsuit and warm mittens and boots. After I harnessed up the six dogs that were raring to go, I set out on a trail that led down to our valley. It was twenty eight below zero and snowing lightly. I kept a close check on my dogs as we roared down the trail at high speed. They were at the peak of freshness, and excited as to what we might see. I did not want any injuries to mar this gorgeous cold day. The filtered sunlight lit up the dog's breath, wrapping us all in a warm haze as we speeded along a top field. Topping a little ridge, just before heading down the drop to the valley hill, I could see drifts ahead in small and large mounds made by the light breeze. Soon something very odd started happening. The snow around the sled and team began exploding in large puffs. I tried braking and braced the sled. I realized prairie chickens had burrowed under the snow drifts and were completely hidden from sight. As the dogs plowed through the drifts, the chickens flew up in surprise at their safe haven being disrupted. My how the dogs reacted! "Alright," 'alright," I yelled, forgetting any thoughts of stopping the team. Where there is one of these birds there are sometimes many. We continued running on through a gate and down the valley hill. Another flurry of snow and my lead dog Takla had lucked on to a bird right in front of her mussel. She did not miss a beat as usual and grabbed it in her mouth and continued running in lead. Another explosion close to Takla, and she dropped the chicken she had and tried for another. Lucky for me she missed it and we continued on our way downhill. Rounding a turn farther down towards our leased land, we saw a huge moose on the loose. He was an enormous fellow and turned his majestic head to look at us. The dogs became wild as they caught his scent. Moose are unpredictable as hell and many dog mushers had stories and scars to tell about after a moose encounter. I did not have a gun but I'd had intentions of taking a fire arms course for certification of handguns soon. I had tried carrying my husband's rifle on the sled but found it was a lot of trouble and awkward. I really hoped I wasn't too late in trying to get a smaller gun. I had been lucky so far in dodging this kind of encounter. The moose looked us over slowly, then turned and headed into the swamp spruce casually, not interested in us THIS time. I breathed a bit easier. It was very unlikely the moose would change direction and bother us. I lifted my foot off the brake and opened up the dogs and let them run past the swamp and onto another dog trail. As we turned more exploding snow and prairie chickens flew up to greet us. Thankfully this time we were not close enough to them, for one of the dogs to catch any. Leaving the swamp, the moose, and the chickens behind, we climbed a huge hill and then entered a broad lane of trees. This took a great deal of energy from the dogs and they were settling in to the pace and looking quite mellow.

I came to a place on the trail where I often stopped to feed squirrel a few peanuts I carried with me. The squirrels had became quite tame and kept their distance from the dogs but allowed me to approach and feed them goodies. I pulled over with a "Whoa," as my dogs could probably use a bit of a break after the excitement of the chickens, the moose, and the big hill. We had been on the trail for quite some time and it was starting to get dark. As I got off the sled to feed my friend the squirrel, I found no need to restrain the team as they usually waited quite nicely for me. I had just finished feeding the bushy tail and returning to the sled, when the snow exploded in front of the team of dogs. My athletes were still excited and bolted after the wayward bird. With a flying lunge I managed to grab hold of a runner. The dogs drug me a good fifty yards before they finally stopped. Staggering to my feet and clutching a sprained wrist, I ordered my mischievous pals onward. The dogs and I emerged back onto the trail at the top of the valley hill and we all headed for home in the dark. I swear I could see the dogs grinning as we pulled into the home place. Upon feeling my frozen face I realized that I too had a big smile on my face. After taking the harnesses off my pals, I went in search of warm buckets of food for them. After all they would need energy for tomorrow's trip.

Chapter Four

Hunter's
May Be Dangerous

It was a bright sunny fall day and I was returning home from work with my preschool kids. The days were long at the Child development Centre in Dawson Creek. I could hardly wait to get home and head out with my team of dogs on the summer cart we had built. It was hard to tell who was happier the dogs or me. What a gorgeous fall day to head out and see the wonderful colors and have some quiet time looking at nature and wilderness. I threw on a pair of jeans under my summer dress for warmth and harnessed up the lot. We were off to a fast start and I decided to take a journey down to the bottom lease and check out our little herd of beef cows that we have. The sun was warm on my face and the dogs trotted along at a nice pace, heads up looking for game. We leisurely made our way around and through the cattle, making sure all was well. Then I decided to return on a back trail to a little meadow down in the bottom of our little valley. We popped out of the bush and a flash of reflective light hit me in the eyes. It seemed like sun reflecting off glass. We were about three hundred yards from a red pickup truck pulling a small wagon with a four wheel quad on it. It was sitting to the side of our little meadow. Standing beside the truck was a man in camouflage hunting gear with a rifle and scope to his shoulder pointed straight at me and my dogs. My heart quickened its pace and I felt the breath go out of me. I was just sure a shot would ring out and would take down one of the dogs or me. Takla my leader was black and some of these hunters will shoot anything that moves. I hadn't thought to ever be in this position, as we own the property and most respectable hunters ask permission to hunt, so we know when they are on our land. It took us just a few seconds to speed across the meadow but it felt like two hours and I kept listening for a shot. The fellow must have caught a glimpse of my face in his scope. I am absolutely sure I looked as terrified as I felt. He ran and jumped into the truck, and pulled a U turn, and away he went. He ripped out of the little valley as if he was on fire. I followed in mad pursuit my team wide open. The hunter looked in his rearview mirror a tried to put a little more lead on the gas, but he was on a rough country trail and the dogs and I were gaining ground. The cart flew as we raced along and the dust flew up and made it hard to see. I kept urging the dogs on and the hunter fled in distress as he was staring at six very fast mutts and a very mad driver. We finally hit the road by our home place and the dust was flying up so much I nearly missed the driveway. The hunter sped on by, now he was on a better road he could go a lot faster. I was extremely scared, mad, and half crying as I pulled the dogs up to the workshop where my son Dan., who was skinny, seventeen and in work overalls was working on his pride and joy, his old ford pickup truck. He asked me which way the hunter had went and I told him. He said "I'll catch him with my ford." He got in his truck and flew out the driveway after the fleeing hunter, who by this time was a few miles down the road. About five miles later, almost to our community hall he caught sight of the hunter's truck pulling the wagon. Dan sped up and while overtaking him pointed for him to pull over. The hunter thought something was wrong with his wagon so he pulled to the side and stopped as he did not associate Dan with the scoping incident. Dan weighing in at about one hundred pounds and ripped a strip off that hunter like you wouldn't believe. He made sure the guy knew how badly he had scared me and that he had no permission to be on the property. He also informed him that I drove my dogs there every day and if he ever saw him even close to our property he would not only be in jail, but nursing many wounds. The hunter apologized but my son did not have a lot of sympathy as he told him if he had pulled the trigger I would be dead, and then what are you going to do. It is against the law in B.C. to scope a human with a firearm.

I was waiting patiently at the house when Dan returned. He got out of his fast ford and was shaking almost as much as me. He told me about the conversation he had with the hunter and also added the hunter probably weighed in at two hundred and fifty pounds and could have knocked him down in one swat. I guess there is something to be said for the little guy trying to protect his Mom. Dan said "Well, that guy was dead wrong and he knew it." I thought about that scope on me and said "I was almost dead, right."

Chapter Five

The Mad Moose

My dogs loved to run in the early morning at first light. This was not always possible as I worked full time on week days and usually hit the trail about four thirty pm., or later in the afternoon.

One winter on a Saturday morning we harnessed up and hit the trail at daybreak. The trail we had been using was a well packed trail. My husband used a small tractor with chains, pulling a log and this hard packed a great trail down to my little valley, where numerous trails awaited us. This was a winter where we had a great amount of snowfall. The team did not like to get off the packed trail as it was quite a struggle to get moving in the deep snow and a hundred times harder to pull a sled.

The dogs were fresh and raring to go so we headed onto the packed trail that snaked across a field. Occasionally I'd day dreamed about entering the sled dog races in the Ft. John and Charlie lake area, as I knew my dogs were fast, as I had timed them on long haul races. I am not really a serious competitor but I knew along with others, that my team was fast and very quick. On one occasion when I attended a race in Tumbler Ridge my dogs were a full minute ahead of the popular local champion.

Soaring down the packed trail was heaven on earth and I was content running my dogs without expectations of winning races. The only thing I could hear was their panting breath, and the swish and glide of the runners on the trail. I fully enjoyed the sheer exhilaration of flying along the path, and the freedom of the moment, when the dogs leaned into the harness and picked the speed up even more. We shot ahead faster than ever, and the dogs were wild with excitement.

Up ahead I could see something on the trail. There was something that was large and black causing the dogs to react. I tried to brake the sled gently, at this high speed, but the dogs worked together, all in agreement to surge forward. By this time I could see a large black cow moose directly ahead and right in the middle of our trail. She wasn't moving off the trail into the deep snow. Not for anything would she wade into that deep mess.

She turned and came toward us a slow but determined trot. My dogs were wildly excited and out of control. I decided to do what the experienced mushers told me to do in such circumstances. I braked again and tipped the sled over into the very deep snow at the edge of the packed trail. The moose was only about a hundred yards away. The sudden braking and overturning of my sled, catapulted me onto my butt in the snow a couple of yards behind the sled. The dogs had stopped and were looking back at me in amazement. This was enough for the old cow moose to begin a charge. In a few split seconds she was right on the dogs. She did not stop to stomp on them but kicked and tromped on what she could as she made her way off the packed trail into the hip deep snow. Dumbfounded I watched her head off toward the bush, the snow nearly up to her shoulders.

I regained my feet shakily and began to examine my poor dogs. Takla my leader had a skinned nose and front leg. Yacoom my big wheel dog had blood oozing out of his nose. Trixie had a large rip on her ear and was whining. Old Tundra also had blood seeping out her ear. What a disaster. Not knowing how serious the injuries were, I turned everyone loose but little Takla who was still ready to pull and wanted to go in the direction of the cow moose. I come geed (full right turn) the sled, and headed for home walking behind the sled. Behind me, the line of casualties, all in single file limping along.

We finally made it home just as it was getting dark. After close examination no one was seriously injured. We were certainly lucky to escape with minor cuts and bruises. I cleaned up the sad looking lot as were really, extremely lucky.

For the next six weeks I enrolled in a hand gun training program through the Northern lights College. I also purchased a forty four magnum Smith and Wesson gun to carry on the sled. When I enrolled in the program I was the only woman amongst twenty men. They all seemed very amused until exam day. I scored higher on the practical test and higher on the written exam than any of them. The instructor stated that a lot of men although they have had a lot of experience with guns pick up bad habits and have a hard time correcting them, and quite often women with little experience learn it right, the first time.

My plan now was to scare off the moose with a couple shots, if I got into a tricky situation again, but if

I had to I would shoot it. There are times when you have to shoot to defend life and property. If this happens it is a good idea to call authorities and salvage any meat. Many people thought it amusing that I carried my gun but should a team tangle with a moose or a bear, you are powerless to stop them. Shooting in the air may drive them away or you may have to kill them. I realized how much I had to learn about this sport but also how much I was learning daily.

This same winter we had another moose incident. The snow was really deep and we had one old dog Tasha who was fifteen years old, involved in a mad scramble with a cow moose.

We had set out several, large, round hay bales for our beef calves, not too far behind Tasha's dog house. A cow moose came up to the bales with her yearling calf, and started eating the hay. Tasha spotted them and started barking madly to chase them away. The cow left the calf eating hay and began to lure Tasha into the deeper snow to stomp on her. Tasha would venture off the packed snow around her dog house, barking frantically, and the cow moose would charge her. She would scramble madly back through the deep snow to a packed area, barley missing being tromped on by the cow. The snow was so deep the dog looked like she was swimming through it. She would run back and forth on the packed, hard snow, and then venture forth into the deeper snow again. The old cow would wait until she got quite a ways in, and then take another run at her. Poor old Tasha, stiff and arthritic, would just barely make it back to safety. The big calf casually continued eating hay, while mama moose protected his supper. This war between dog and moose continued on for about an hour, while the calf munched on his supper. By this time old Tasha was played out and getting slower to retreat. I held my breath as time after time, the poor old dog managed to barely escape.

Finally mama moose must have decided baby had enough to eat and they moseyed on out of there. I was happy to seem them go as I feared for my dog's life. She had been getting slower at each charge of the moose.

Chapter Six

Merry Go Round

Takla was our teams little speed queen. She always had fun on any trip. She held her head up, was always alert to where on the trail she was, and bounded along at a blistering pace.

One January day, I hooked up the team and was ready to go. I was suited out in my warmest snowsuit and rabbit fur hat. On my feet were white Sorrel snow packs that were warm to minus forty degrees. My warm mittens had three layers and I had a nice neck warmer that made a difference, as it could be pulled up over the face if the wind was cold.

It was a very bitter day at minus thirty two degrees as we headed down a packed field trail to a bottom side hill. The team was fresh and we made tracks in the fresh snow as we sped along the trail.

The dogs had rested all day waiting for the chance to explore and were picking up the pace well, on the trail. A thread of excitement ran through the team as they caught the scent of some elk in the bush to our right. A big cow elk and yearling calf lunged out of sight as we rounded a curve. The elk were so elusive. All we caught was a glimpse of them. As we headed through a narrow trail we could see several other cow elk in the poplar trees. We continued our way down the narrow trail. It was a very still and quiet. I could hear the dogs puffing and the swish of the sled's runners on the hard snow. We were about twenty yards into a new trail when I turned my head to the side and looked directly into the eyes of something crouched on a fallen log. I turned my head to see it as we passed and realized it was a lynx, a large cat commonly called a bobcat. My dogs were totally unaware that they had passed the large cat. The lynx did not move and was so well camouflaged that the dogs did not see or smell it.

Plowing along the trail my sled picked up a stick and it managed to get lodged underneath it somehow. I stopped the dogs and began to try to loosen the stick. My patient intelligent leader waited and held the team in check. The stick was fairly large and I couldn't seem to get it out. Finally with the team restrained but eager to run, and after ten minutes of struggling, the stick broke loose. I gave a big yell and said "right on." The dogs took this for the signal "hike on' and away they went leaving me looking after them in amazement. I was a long way from home and it was bitter cold out although I was warmly and properly dressed. Well, I thought, I'll just have to walk home. I walked in my heavy snow boots and warm layered clothing for ten minutes and my eyelashes and nose were getting covered with frost. I was not looking forward to the climb up the hill out of the valley. Suddenly I felt like something was behind me. Slowly I turned to see if the big cat I had previously seen or another form of wildlife was stalking me. To my surprise and approaching fast was my team of dogs and sled. The dogs had made a full circle at the top of the hill and hit another trail and came up behind me. I hailed them down to a stop and literally danced onto the runners. We continued on up the steep hill and it was like nothing had happened. I was very careful about shouting things that might be mistaken for a signal after that. Lesson learned.

This merry go round also happened to my husband as he had borrowed my dogs to go on a fencing expedition. When you raise beef cattle, fences need to be fixed and the dogs were an easy access to the fences in the summer via the dog cart. It was a sunny day in July and Carl set out with my team of dogs to repair fence lines. He stopped and became engrossed in splicing up some wire. The dogs were fresh as a daisy and he stopped on a trail that had some potential of wildlife being spotted on it. This was too much temptation for my mischievous friends and away they went leaving him behind. He continued his fencing job and repaired a good deal of fence line, when the dogs and cart came loping back to where he was. They had not got tangled up, nor were had they upset or drug the cart. They were looking at him as if to say, "Are you finished yet, let's go?" He was very glad he did not have to walk home. Yikes! What a merry go round!

Chapter Seven

Trixie Bogs Down

Trixie my silky little Eskimo dog was a scrappy little dog who worked to her full potential in the harness. She was a small little girl but her downfall was her big, loose hairy feet. Her feet never were sore, as the hair between the toes protected the delicate areas. However, the hair also collects snow and when the snow is warm, can collect snow balls.

On one occasion we set off on the trail in mid morning. Things were going well and the weather was warming up from a minus twelve to a balmy plus two degrees.

We had been travelling a our normal rapid speed as the dogs were in good physical shape and were enjoying the run when I began to notice little Trixie was getting very tired, and began slowing up, causing the other dogs to become annoyed at her. They were giving her warning and growling wanting her to pick up her pace. I knew something was wrong with her, so I stopped and anchored the dogs. Unfortunately, the warm weather had caused the snow to ball up and cling to her silky fur. The extra weight was becoming heavy and uncomfortable and causing her to become exhausted, not to mention her lagging back was causing her problems with her team mates who had no tolerance for slackers.

I tried cleaning her feet and letting her continue in the harness but the snow would build up and ball up on her feet rapidly, and the other dogs were turning on her in frustration.

I finally stopped the sled and removed her harness, and turned her loose. She still lagged behind us. When we finally returned home she had huge balls of snow clinging to her feet. My other dog's feet were fine as they had small, tight feet, resistant to the wet snow.

This happened before and I learned the hard way that to run this little dog in the warmer weather, she needed to wear booties of thick durable material. This magically solved the warm weather problem.

Chapter Eight

Coyote in the Woodshed

After a long run with dogs on a very cold day I went to feed the dogs. They had worked hard and it was cold so I had previously made up buckets of nutritious food.

I used a commercial feed of good quality for the main staple. This main feed was thirty five percent quality protein and fifteen percent fat. This feed is not cheap but if dogs are working hard they need a high quality main food as they burn up to eight thousand calories a day. I would cook rice or oats as a carbohydrate, add the commercial feed along with chicken fat or corn oil. This helped the animals maintain a healthy coat, skin, and feet. On this particular day in February I had added a little good beef tallow to the mush and it smelt very yummy, even to me a hungry driver.

My dogs were chained beside their individual dog houses with the exception of Yacoom, my big, husky,

Doreen E. Wolff

wheel dog who was laying in the work shop on a bed. I walked out with a feed pail in hand, to Takla the lead dog's dog house and began spooning mush into her dish. Out from behind a near willow brush came a coyote, teeth bared and on the move towards the food and I. It was not more than six feet away, when a bark and a vicious growl came from a blur of black and grey fur hurtling between myself and the coyote. My big friend Yacoom had saved the day. He chased the miserable coyote into the nearest shed which was an open three sided woodshed. There he kept it, and ran back and forth to keep it trapped in. The coyote tried every means of escape possible.

First the sneaky coyote tried jumping over the barking dog. Yacoom caught him in mid air and through him back in the woodshed. Then he tried digging under the wall at the back of the woodshed. He had no luck with his digging under the wall, as the ground was frozen stiff. He tried to out smart the dog with quick moves, but the big old dog could really move and out foxed him every time. I watched and had a good laugh as this fellow coyote was not as smart as he had figured he was, and he had certainly met his match now. Finally the coyote found a break in the plywood wall of the shed and managed to squeeze through a little three or four inch space. He was scratched and bleeding but took off as fast as he could with the dog in pursuit.

Two hours later, the big husky finally returned. He was exhausted from chasing that coyote over hill and dale. Lunging through that deep snow was like swimming in very deep and thick water and my poor old friend was pretty tired for the rest of the day. One thing I do know is that he gave that despicable coyote a run for his money.

Chapter Nine

The Big Cat

On a fine summer day my dogs and I hit the trail with the dog cart. My lead dog Takla, had worked hard and she had gained respect and affection from me, as well as respect and obedience from her teammates. She could be depended on to keep the line tight and knew if anyone fell off the cart or sled. She was a great help in managing the dogs on a summer cart, as it is an awesome task. She was a genius at sniffing out and spotting game along the trail.

On this particular day Takla did not seem to be herself, as we approached a pond on a flat, in a valley. I glanced at my big wheel dog, and the fur on his neck was standing on end and he seemed very nervous. The other dogs on the team were picking up signals from the first two and also began acting strange.

The dogs began side stepping along the steep hill towards the pond, very nearly upsetting the cart and dumping me off. We skirted closer to the pond and I began feeling what the dogs were feeling, as if something strange and unfamiliar was watching us.

The team ignoring my precise directions, were straining against their harness, toward a stand of small poplar trees by the pond. On closer examination I could see the bull rushes moving along the banks of the pond as if something was sneaking along. Some birds flew up and lit out of there and scared me. The lure of a chase inherited from their ancestors, made the team on the cart hard to control. I jumped on the brake with such force I heard something snap but I managed to slow the lot of them down to a crawl.

Out of the grass and bull rushes leapt a giant cougar. The enormous cat sprang up and straight out of the deep depression by the stand of trees beside the pond. The long tail of the big cat was straight out and there was no mistaking this was the real thing, not anything my dogs or I wanted to deal with. The dogs needed no urging to get back on the trail fast as they seemed to think the chase was on. The cougar had disappeared into the trees without a trace and we pursed the cart trail with a racing speed never before found on the cart.

I regained my courage and kept the dogs on track. We made it home after our journey in a gear we had never achieved before.

The dogs never forgot the exact spot we had seen the cougar by that pond. Each and every time I passed close to that area, their noses and heads would come up. The excitement and alertness showed me they wanted another glimpse of the big cat.

Chapter Ten

Christmas Brawl

Once in awhile the dogs would have to work out the pecking order. Takla, the female lead dog was always dominant and showed her control over the team. Most of the hard working dogs leaned into the harness and did a super pulling job, and they did not like a lazy fellow team mate. The team would show aggression to one dog in particular. This was little Trixie, a small unseasoned female was in danger of a reprimand from Takla the leader. Every once in awhile Trixie would trip over lines or seize any opportunity, a tangle or a dip to sit down and rest. When Takla would let a dog know it needed to smarten up, all the rest of the team backed her up, and snarled, bit, nipped and ripped, the unlucky slacker. I drove a dog named Toby for awhile, a huge male, supposedly half wolf, but he was extremely lazy and the team and myself could not put up with him. The team however accepted little Trixie but they would get on her case to go faster and stop less. She got better in time, as she was getting seasoned in, and began gaining strength and stamina. She also had some foot problems as she had large hairy feet. Her feet tended to collect snow when it was warm and this would slow her down. Her feet never were sore or lame. If it was too warm the use of booties solved the problem so we put up with the little gal. She however was quite timid and submissive, as the reaction was out of fear. Trixie was actually quite a timid but yappy dog. On the whole she knew her place in the team. I tolerated some of these things because my dogs had become such great pets.

It was two weeks before Christmas in 1999. My daughter, Karen and son-in-law Mike, were living quite close at this time, in near by Dawson Creek. They were very soon expecting their first child to arrive. We all decided to get live spruce trees to decorate for Christmas and to go as a family together.

Mike was anxious to try driving the dog team, so I decided to let him have a go at driving the dogs. The rest of us could take the 4X4 truck. We did not have a lot of snow that winter, so we all decided to venture down to a bottom valley where there were some bushy spruce trees.

The dogs were fresh and extremely hyper but we harnessed them up. I was sure Mike had seen me drive enough that he'd be O.K. and the dogs knew the way even if he didn't. It was a hard packed, icy trail through a field, onto a lease, and into a stand of spruce and pine trees. Mike weighed in at about two hundred pounds and would probably slow the dogs down a bit as they were use to me at one hundred and fifteen pounds. Mike left with a flash of fur teeth, as the dogs felt the driver was different. The rest of us came in the old dodge 4X4 along with the pregnant daughter.

The sled flew down the hill with such a speed I am sure the runners were smoking hot. Mike clung to that sled like a burr to some fur. He sped on through the field and made the lease in jig time. We were right behind in the dodge, and all managed to pull into a trail in the group of evergreens. The dogs were very excited but I tied them up to a tree because we had found a couple of nice spruce that would make great Christmas trees.

We were just getting the chain saw to take down a couple trees when all hell broke loose. The excited dogs not use to being tied up, when they were so fresh were in a mad and dangerous fight. Takla and the other female Tundra had little Trixie by the ears and they meant business. Yacoom was watching every thing and keeping his cool, but little Trixie made an aggressive move toward Takla the lead dog and punctured her nose. Yacoom lost his cool and jumped on Trixie and had her by the throat. Tundra and Takla both jumped on little Trixie too. All that I could see was a mass of snarling, biting, yelping fur and teeth. Dog drivers have been bitten in fights, serious facial scarring, and too many injuries to even think about, but my pregnant daughter waded into the mess and grabbed Takla and Tundra uptight. Mike finally had Trixie but she was locked onto Takla'as nose. I had grabbed Yacoom who was really very disciplined through all of this. Trixie was finally pulled loose and I could see a fair amount of blood coming from her, from some good sized gashes. Mike finally had Trixie unsnapped from the tugline,

I surveyed the damage to see who was fit to run. It seemed like the whole team was O.K. but had a few gashes that were not serious except for little Trixie who was beat up pretty badly. She had taken a bad beating from the three others near her. She was not fit to run so I loaded her in the dodge for a ride home and repair to her injuries. Everyone else I hooked back up and felt the run home would do them good and settle them down. The rest of the family stayed and finished taking down the Christmas trees and came back with Trixie, a bit later.

After I got back to the farm and unhooked the dogs, I washed and cleaned the injuries putting ointment on the lacerations and punctures. After this little Trixie never offered to challenge the other dogs but knew her place in the team. Takla would just look at her and lift a lip in a snarl and Trixie would pick up the pace remarkably, head down in submission.

The family refers to this incident as "The Christmas Brawl." I must confess it was my fault, as every good musher knows, never tie your dogs up together, when they are raring to go. I still wonder what we would have done if the pregnant lady would have went into labor! It might have got interesting!!

Chapter Eleven

Up Close With Mama Black Bear

It was September and we headed out on an adventure to enjoy the fall colors and the hint of crispness in the air. The dogs were fresh and ready to explore new trails and see what game was about on this wonderful autumn day.

We snaked through the rocky creek bed and onto a small hay field. Crossing a gravel road and looking both ways we went into an oat field with a dirt trail down one side. The dirt trail went up and down over little gullies and little hills.

My big dog Yacoom was running loose with the team as he was new and had not built up pulling stamina yet. The dog cart breezed along at top speed. We came over a little rolling hill almost on top of a mama black bear! I caught a glimpse of two black cubs, eating oats to my left.

Mama bear was not a happy camper and took a swat at Yacoom, knocking him end over end. He was yipping and whining like he was hurt. I kept my cool and ordered the team to "come gee." Making a U turn to the right, we quickly headed back in the direction we had came. Yacoom had picked himself up and ran behind us as we rushed full speed for home. I never looked back.

We pulled into the home place and I checked Yacoom for injuries. He had nothing wrong but the daylights scared out of him.

My husband Carl and his friend were working in the shop and I related what had happened. They decided to go and take a look at the bears in the 4X4 truck. When they returned they informed me that the bears had moved a little farther away, into another oat field where there were no dogs to bother their fall preparation for hibernation. They had counted not two cubs but three cubs.

Chapter Twelve

Not so Elusive Elk

In the area where I drove the dogs the most, elk were in abundance. It was not remarkable to see forty,or more elk in a hay field. They were not well liked by ranchers or farmers as the gobbled up the grain and were hard on hay bales and stacks. Moose will eat on one bale at a time but elk tramp and urinate on all bales in a hay stack making it not eatable for livestock. Most local people used reindeer fence to fence off bale stacks from these hungry fellows

One of the most unique experiences with the dog team is with a herd of elk during a terrific snow storm. On our excursions we had seen plenty of elk. Sometimes they would wait a few minutes and move on, and other times they were elusive and you would just catch a glimpse of them. They were very quick to disappear when the cows had young calves with them and the bulls we never saw at all.

The dogs and I had travelled a long ways on the trail, when the snow that had been falling, began to swirl and a hard northern wind blew it at angle directly into us. The dogs kept their heads down low, looking at the trail and trying to meet the battering wind blowing sleet and snow at us. Turning my head to both sides, I could see numerous elk sheltering from the storm. They were on both sides of the trail, hunkered down and waiting patiently for the storm to pass. Some of these elk were so close I could see them blinking and closing their eyes to protect them from the icy pellets that were blasting them.

My dogs seemed unaware of how close they were to the elk, and the elk were likewise unaware of the dogs. We all moved together at a slow pace, travelling downhill in the punishing wind and snow. It was like a dream as we wove our way through the trees only ten to twenty feet away from the elk. We moved like a unit through the bush as if we were in a dream. This continued for about half an hour until the trail reached a field. Here the dogs continued but the elk stayed back in the sheltering trees. It was an incredible experience.

Chapter Thirteen

On The Riverboat

On occasion we would take our riverboat out on the northern rivers in British Columbia. One of my favorite rivers to travel on is the Murray River, southwest of our farm.

When my dog Takla was a youngster, we decided to take a trip on the good old Murray River. I felt that Takla deserved a bit of a break too, as I had been working her hard with training and she really liked water. We packed up the gear,and two dogs and with the old boat headed out camping along the Murray River.

When we were in the boat cruising along the river, the dogs loved to ride on the hood, where they could see and smell wildlife. We would cruise along slowly with both dogs riding on the front hood looking at the riverbanks for game, sniffing the air, and loving the motion of the boat.

On this trip we also had friends with boats along and they had told us of a little creek running into the Murray where the fishing was spectacular. After camping overnight, we decided to try out the super fishing spot. We were not quite sure where it was but we knew we would find it.

We were moving down the river at a pretty good clip, the dogs enjoying the breeze and perched on the nose of the boat. We zipped by the mouth of a little creek that ran into the river. There was the super fishing hole so we shut down the throttle so rapidly that Takla tumbled out and under the splashing water at the front of the boat and the boat passed completely over her. This was not a small aluminum boat but a big old heavy riverboat! We travelled up and down the area for six minutes or so, looking for my poor little pooch. Finally I spotted her running up and down on the rocks on the bank, looking confused and disoriented. We pulled into shore and I jumped out and called for her but she was in shock and dazed and kept running back and forth. I am sure she had a concussion and she certainly had confusion. I finally got hold of her and calmed her down.

The next day Takla was back to her old self, but she never forgot that incident and was always very cautious around water the rest of her life. I also never forgot the incident and would not let the dogs ride on the front of the boat anymore, no matter how much they enjoyed it. Live and learn. Learn and live.

Chapter Fourteen

The Diagnosis

In the middle of October of 2003, I began having periods of low energy and tiredness. I constantly felt exhausted and drained. It took all my effort to get up in the morning and shower. Cooking dinner took so much effort and sapped so much energy that I would have to sit down and rest. People began telling me I looked tired. I finally made an appointment with my doctor but felt I hardly needed a physical exam as I was pretty regular in my check ups. To be honest I was happy to go as I was sick of feeling tired and felt some vitamins might give me some needed energy. Better safe than sorry.

After a quick check-in, I was led to an examination room. Doctor P. Boronowski asked questions about history, and then got down to business. All the while we chatted about other things such as gardening, dogs, farming, horses, and weather. This doctor had been my friend and doctor for over twenty five years. Thirty minutes later he was recommending radiology and ultrasounds. I had my last mammogram on time and everything had been fine. I was sent to the Dawson Creek General hospital for the tests as he seemed concerned about my underarms, ribs and breasts.

After reading all the articles in the waiting room at the hospital I was given a series of many tests. The radiologist examined the results, and I was told to wait. I was asked if any family was with me and Dr. Boronowski was called over to the hospital from his office.

Together after examining the results, I was given a needle biopsy. I was feeling very nervous by this time. I was told that there was suspicion of breast cancer in the ribs and lymph glands and that the confirmation would take one week to ten days. I stood in shock realizing how little else mattered but your health. I had did everything right. I had regular mammograms, exercise, eating healthy, and not smoking. I felt I had a very healthy lifestyle and was very furious that this could happen to me.

For a brief period of time I was in denial. I told myself the tests were sure to come back clear and the ten day waiting period seemed like a year.

My doctor's office phoned me at work a t the Child Development Centre where I worked with young children, and asked me to come immediately, to the office for a conference about the results of the test and to bring a family member, or friend if I felt I needed support. I was terrified but away I went feeling like the wind was knocked out of me. I was quickly shown into a conference room when I arrived at the doctor's office.

Upon taking a seat, the doctor and his wonderful nurse Peggy, entered with folders and booklets. I watched as their usual happy faces, turned to very serious and worried expressions. They exchanged grim looks and began going over the results of the many tests. The diagnosis was stage three breast cancer, already spread to the lymph nodes. We looked at X-rays and made another appointment to talk about my "options." Driving home, the thirty minutes to the farm, my emotions were threatening to consume me. I went from anger to worrying about my kids. Then I began crying, praying, and promising to get through this thing.

Upon returning home the thing I remember most vividly was hooking up my dogs and the peace and freedom of the trail that day.

I continued running my team of dogs in the rest of October, until the diagnosis was confirmed. In November we met with the general doctor and surgeon and discussed chemotherapy and radiation. The only time I relaxed was during my dog sledding adventures, which took my mind off my problems and made me treasure every trip.

Chapter Fifteen

The Surgery and The Treatment

On the first week of January, now 2004, I underwent surgery in the Dawson Creek General hospital. With incisions in my ribs and incisions under both armpits my adventures with the dogs were put on hold. My spirits were very low during this time and I was physically very sore and in pain from the surgery. I was starting to lose hope and wondered what the future had in store for me. When ever I would dream I would dream of the adventures with the dogs and the freedom and peace of mind my excursions gave me.

My old friend Yacoom barked excitedly at me one day in mid winter. He was asking me to harness him up and go out on the trail. With my arms and ribs feeling much better but not completely healed, I managed to harness up four dogs, and I was off. Viewing the white-tailed deer in the woods and seeing them wave their tails in good-bye made me thankful to be alive.

Next, I was sent to Grande Prairie, Alberta to undergo chemotherapy treatment. Grande Prairie is approximately two hours from our farm, but specialized in chemo treatments for our area, and we were able to travel the four hour round trip so I could stay at home. I was not able to take the anti nausea pills given to me and experienced periods of extreme nausea. My immunity became very low and in order to take the chemo I had to daily take shots in my stomach to build it up in order to continue the treatments. I became very weak in body and in spirits.

In February of 2004, I was hardly able to walk twenty feet but, pulling a toque over my bald head, and putting on my snowsuit, I managed somehow to hook up the fantastic foursome and headed out. The peace and solitude of the trail gave me new hope and my friends the four dogs, made me laugh at their antics. Sniffing the air in joy and almost smiling with their freedom, we went for many miles before returning to the farm. Once back after many miles it was easy to take off the harnesses, as the dogs were totally pooped out. I had returned home with the most wonderful sense of well being and accomplishment.

I continued to run my dogs throughout my treatment and battle with cancer. They became my blessing and my freedom, and my way of escape out of a situation I did not want to be in.

I finally became too weak to ride the winter sled. I decided to hook up the dogs and harness them to our four wheel quad. I had learned that some professional mushers used this method to train dogs in the summer. I used this method in the winter on packed smooth trails and fields. On packed trails the dogs could run freely and not have to pull my weight. My advantage is if I saw a moose or a deer that the dogs wanted to chase, I could brake and certainly stop them. I was also quite snug and warm on the quad with the handle warmers.

Throughout this time my dogs became my best friends and support. They seemed to know I was sick. Three of the four dogs could nearly harness themselves! They would stick their heads in the harness and then lift their front feet into the appropriate holes. My big boy Yacoom never did learn this trick but had to be helped each and every time.

On the trail the dogs would slow down when it was rough and look back at me making sure I was alright. When I ran into trouble on the trail my dogs would be calm and try to help out the situation instead of being the former hyper trouble makes they use to be. It really did seem they knew I was weaker and needed their help. It is possible they could smell it as some dog owners tell me this is possible.

As my treatment progressed, and was nearing completion, I rarely missed a day without travelling with my dogs. During my weaker times I used the quad as a sled. The dogs did not mind as they were happy to get out on the trails in any form. They seem to need the work and the peace on the trail as much as I did.

After finishing the chemo treatment I began to regain some of my strength and realized how important these trips were to my physical and mental health. My dogs had became my best friends, the ones who knew me at my strongest and my weakest moments. They had built my confidence in my ability to fight cancer and were my strongest support.

After regaining some of my strength, my old pals were back up to their tricks again. Leaving me dumped off in the snow to walk home after surprising a moose, being hard to harness, and being so fast and excited they were out of control. I felt pretty good about it. It was as if they were telling me they knew I was back to my old self.

The next step in my treatment was six weeks of radiation treatment in Edmonton, Alberta. This is about an eight hour trip, one way, from our farm one way. There was no way I could stay at home and take these treatments. I underwent the radiation treatment at The Cross Cancer Hospital. The staff was very nice and their were seminars to help build your self image such as "look well, feel well."

The thing I missed most was the adventures on the wild trails with my dogs and the dogs themselves. Their affection and mischievous personalities were things I looked forward to, every second week-end when we returned home. By this time it was June and we were able to take the dogcart on our trips into the woods.

Chapter Sixteen

Still going Strong

I have been cancer free now for over five years. This is awesome thing for someone they diagnosed as only having a thirteen percent chance of survival. Almost all of my dogs have gone to the happy sledding trails in the sky. I lost my old friend Yacoom last summer to old age. He was seventeen years old and had a good long life on the trails. The only living survivor of my first dog team is Takla my spirited tough little leader. She is also seventeen years old and is deaf and arthritic but can still get excited about a trip down a trail to the forest. She also tries to get her trotting pace going when she heads out. She is a priceless treasure.

I have had no return of the cancer but when I feel a panic attack of fear of it returning, and becoming sick again, I think of my dogs and all the adventures on the trail we've has. These adventures have been a great part of my life story. No-one knows the ending to their own story, but we should all know the importance of living each day to the fullest.

The feel of the wind in your hair, the glide of a sled over a new snowfall, the beauty of snowflakes falling in a stand of spruce trees, the excitement of the chase of a deer or moose, the annoyance of a mischievous dog friend is what I have enjoyed in my life. I wouldn't have missed it for the world!